THE BETRAYAL OF A MAN

THE BETRAYAL OF A MAN

TABITHA R. MATHIS

To order additional copies of this book, contact:
Xlibris Corporation
1-888-795-4274
www.Xlibris.com
Orders@Xlibris.com
76362

CONTENTS

Acknowledgments... 11

Introduction.. 13

Chapter 1

How We Met.. 15

Chapter 2

Our First Date... 19

Chapter 3

A Hater Move 25

Chapter 4

Showing Some Love 28

Chapter 5

The Big Fight.. 33

Chapter 6

Happy Birthday... 42

Chapter 7

Entering Womanhood 47

Chapter 8

Busted in Action 50

Chapter 9

The Big Day 57

Chapter 10

The Betrayal... 61

A SPECIAL DEDICATION TO ALL YOUNG TEENAGERS ACROSS THE WORLD. BE WISE IN EVERYTHING YOU DO. DON'T LET ANY MEN RUN GAME ON YOU. EDUCATION IS THE KEY TO LIFE. ALWAYS FOLLOW YOUR DREAMS. PUT GOD FIRST BEFORE EVERYTHING. MEN COME AND GO. YOU ALWAYS HAVE ENOUGH TIME TO HAVE KIDS. ENJOY LIFE FIRST!

THANKS,

MS. TABITHA MATHIS

WHO IS AS THE WISE MAN?
AND WHO KNOWETH THE
INTERPRETATION OF A THING?
A MAN" S WISDOM MAKETH
HIS FACE TO SHINE AND THE
BOLDNESS OF HIS FACE SHALL
BE CHANGED.

ECCLESIASTES 8:1

ACKNOWLEDGMENTS

God, I want to thank you for being the head in my life. I want to thank you for blessing me with four beautiful children—Quintavious, Quaiesha, JaQwaiveyon, and LaKwambria Mathis. I thank you, Lord, for my special friend Anthony Smith.

I want to give thanks to my mom, Eva Mathis, for having me and not giving up on me. Thanks to my stepfather, Mr. George T. Sands, for being that father I needed.

I would love to thank my fourth-grade teacher Mrs. Juanita Smith for teaching me how to write poetry. Your thought will never be forgotten.

Lord, bless my sisters Georgina and Tiffany Mathis; also, bless my brother, Vincent Brown. Gina, keep on being a good mom and don't give up on your dreams.

A special thanks to Mr. Van Bryant a.k.a. Thrill. You truly inspired me in many ways. Every time I was sad, you lifted me up.

Through thick and thin, also in muddy waters, I would love to thank my best friend Jacqueline Douglas. We have been friends for twenty-three years. God bless you, sis.

Lord, bless my brothers Morley Bryant, James Sands, Sylvester Squire III, Shawn Brown, and Jakaya Hughley (RIP). Thanks for your love and support in our younger days.

To my sister in Christ Pastor Connie Riley, thanks for your encouraging words. I love you, sis.

Lord, bless Aunt Vera Mae Smith who's eighty-five years old. Thanks for guiding me down the right path. A special thanks to my second mother, Mrs. Linda Brady.

Shavoskee Clark, don't work too hard and keep your head up.

I want to thank Ms. Tara Johnson for your love and support.

A special thought to my new sister in Christ, Ms. Melissa Bryant. May God continue to bless you and your family.

I appreciate Mr. Darnelle for being a true friend to me. May God continue to bless you.

Lakwanza McDowell, Anthony Dean, Albert Miller, Travis Snow, Angelia Squire, April Adams, Denise Franklin Carter, Morris Carter, Marciett McKiver, Roshana Banks, Terlina Wadley, Quentin Madison, and Pastor Toru Dean may the lord strengthen you all and keep you all under his wings.

Lord, bless my friends Netarsha Gibson and Audrey McIntyre.

To the one I admired most, Mr. Johnny C. Brady, keep your head up and don't look backward.

May the Lord continue to bless every name on this page in Jesus's name, *amen*!

INTRODUCTION

I am Taquasia. I am dark skinned, pretty, and sexy. I have long shiny black hair. I am from the most popular city in Florida. You can visit the most beautiful beaches. The city I am from has real live flamingos standing on one leg. My city is known for making rap, R&B, and booty-shaking music, baby. We have the most exotic strip clubs you can ever imagine. I am from Miami, Florida. We have the best Caucasian food down here. My mom had four children: Tanzia, Ta'Shontie, and Tonio. I am the oldest of them all.

I had three best friends; their names were Jaliya, Dre, and Tay. Jaliya was skinny, dark skinned, and long-haired. She was her mother's oldest child. She had a lot of jewelry and dressed nice. Dre was in high school. Dre wrestled with his high school wrestling team. He was undefeated. He was also a drug dealer and knew everyone around town. Dre's mother died at a very young age. Tay was the quietest and sneakiest of us all.

I was loved by many, but only chose to love one. At the age of thirteen years old, I met a guy named James. James was handsome, dark skinned, with a six-pack stomach. He wore a rope chain and had a gold grill in his mouth. He drove a purple Lei Vaton Cadillac. He also had a blue BMW and a candy apple red Porsche. James was baller status. He was every young girl's dream. I met James on November 7, 1991. James told me he was in high school. He told me he was eighteen years old. I believed him. He had the most charming eyes to make you believe anything he said.

Chapter 1

How We Met

I was playing outside with my sisters one evening. James walked up to the fence with my best friend Dre.

"What's up, Taquasia? James wanted to speak to you."

"Dre, you're a trip."

"Nah, my dog wanted to holler at you for real."

"Okay, so holler!"

"Hey, Taquasia, I am James."

"Hello, James, how is you?"

"I wanted to pass you my beeper number. You can hit me up anytime, baby, we need to talk. Oh yeah, write my phone number down too. You might want to call me sometimes when you're bored."

"Okay, James, it was nice meeting you."

"It was nice meeting you too."

"Dre, I will talk to you later."

"Okay, Taquasia, we will talk when I come back through. Let me walk James back to the game room."

"All right, Dre, see you when you get back."

I was so excited to meet James. I forgot to ask him his age and where he lived. He was charming to me. I felt my mother wouldn't let me talk to him. I was only thirteen years old. I didn't see Dre for a few days. I never beeped James or called him. On the third day, he came and knocked on my mom's door. My mom answered, "Hi, may I help you?"

"Yes, you may, my name is James," he said, reaching out his hand. "Is Taquasia here?"

"Who?"

"Don't you have a daughter named Taquasia?"

"How do you know my daughter?"

"I met her by her best friend Dre. He sent me to get his jacket for him."

"Oh, okay! Taquasia, come here, baby. Sweetie, a dude named James came to get Dre's coat from you."

"Mom, I already gave it to his sister. I'll go and tell James, okay?"

"Go ahead, sweetie!"

"Hey, James, what's up?"

"How are you, sweetie?"

"Fine, why you came over here?"

"You never did call me."

"I was just waiting on the right time to call you."

"Anytime is the right time for you. I can always make time for my baby."

"How am I your baby already?"

"You are going to be my new girlfriend."

"Why me?"

"You're a special person, you are dark and lovely. I am going to take care of you for the rest of your life. You better believe that."

"That's what you say, action speaks louder than words," I said, smiling.

"I'm going to show you, baby," he said, smiling.

I went back into the house before my mom came out. Momma stopped me at the door, saying, "You stayed out the door longer than I expected. What were you guys talking about?"

"Oh, nothing, Mom, he is cool."

"Don't get knocked out now."

"Yes, ma'am. I am going to my room now."

I went to my room and beeped James. I put my house number behind it. I thought it would make him call back faster. He called back thirty minutes later. I was mad because he didn't call right back. I was happy to hear from him though. I prayed my mom didn't answer the phone at the same time.

"Hey, baby, what's up?"

"Nothing, I just wanted to know, did you mean what you said to me, James?"

"I meant every word. Why don't you believe me, boo?" He smiled. "I'm going to treat you like a queen. You are my queen, and everybody is going to know it."

I had the biggest smile you could ever imagine.

"Taquasia, how you get to school in the mornings?"

"I take the school bus."

"Don't take the school bus in the morning. I want to take you to breakfast, then school."

"How you going to do that?"

"Meet me by the stop sign up the road from your house. What time you have to go to school?"

"I have to be there by 9:00 a.m. What time do you have to go to school, James?"

"Oh, I am going to be late tomorrow."

"You better go to school, boy. I will catch the bus."

"What I said, you my girl now. You don't have to catch the bus anymore."

"Okay, James, whatever you say."

"That's what I'm talking about, baby. I'll call you back before you go to bed."

"All right, James, talk to you later."

"Okay, baby, I'm going to hit you back in a little later. I got to go to work now."

I couldn't wait until the next morning.

I got up early the next morning around 7:00 a.m. I volunteered to walk my sisters to school the next morning. I wanted to be away from the house so I wouldn't get in trouble. I prayed in my head that this guy wouldn't rape me. I also prayed he kept his promise. I was hoping to see Dre so I could talk to him. *I will just wait until I get to school and talk to one of my other friends.* I walked my sisters to school. Guess who I ran into? James. I didn't have to meet him at the stop sign by the house. James was in a candy apple red Porsche.

"What's up, baby? Come give your man a hug." I was kind of nervous, but I hugged him anyway. He opened the car door for me to let me in. I thought it was so cute. He entered the car and kissed my hand. I felt as if I was on cloud 100.

"Taquasia, what's up, baby? Why you so quiet?"

"I don't know."

"Baby, you are beautiful. You have some soft hands. You just quiet and don't like to talk. I'm going to break you out of that."

"Whatever, I like being quiet."

"I want you to talk to me."

"Okay, I'll try to work on talking. I can't promise it will happen soon."

"Take your time, baby. Where do you want to eat at, baby?"

"I would love to go to Denny's."

"Denny's we will go, then."

Chapter 2

Our First Date

While pulling up at Denny's, I was so excited. The restaurant looked so glamorous as if it did on a television commercial. I had never eaten there before. James got out before me to open my side of the car door. He treated me so sweet. He let me order what I wanted to eat. It didn't matter how much the price was. After leaving Denny's, we drove around for a little while before school started. My heart was so thrilled. We pulled up at school. All of the students were out in the front, looking to see who was driving the prettiest Porsche in town.

"Taquasia, are you going to get out without giving me a kiss?" I leaned over and kissed him. I was ready to get out so I could hear what everyone had to say. "I'll pick you up after school. Meet me in the front of the school when you get out."

"James, please be on time."

"I'll be here early to pick up my baby. You will be able to come straight to daddy." I smiled and shut the door. All the students said, "Dang, that car is sharp." I smiled and kept walking, looking for my friends. As I was walking to class, one of the ISS ladies asked me who was that who brought me to school. I told her, "A friend." She said, "He is my husband's cousin." I told her okay and then kept walking.

I still couldn't find my friends. I really wanted to talk to them about my situation. I went on to class. In class, I couldn't concentrate on my lesson. It's as if I was in a daze. Mrs. Ledo's class was always fun and exciting to go to. I just wasn't feeling it that day. James was on my mind all class period. In between changing classes, I saw my best friend Jaliya. I explained to her I needed to talk to her, and it's urgent.

"What is it, Taquasia? Girl, why didn't you catch the bus?"

"I rode to school with my new boyfriend. Jaliya, I have to tell you all about it."

"Who is your new boyfriend? You are keeping me out of the good stuff."

"No, I'm going to tell you. Just make sure you call me tonight."

"Why can't you tell me on the bus?"

"I'm not riding the bus."

"Oh my god, he is picking you up?"

"Yes, girl, now let's get to class. I'll tell all about it later."

"Be careful, sister, you are my best friend. I don't want anything to happen to you."

"Nothing will happen to me. I'll holla at you later."

As I was going to my next class, I was so happy. I felt as if my best friend was happy for me too. I sat down in my next class. All the students were talking about the nice Porsche that brought me to school that morning. I felt good that the students had seen me getting out the Porsche. It made me popular on the same day. One of the boys in my class said, "That's a grown man driving that car." I told him he was lying. He said, "He hangs out with my daddy."

"What is your daddy's name?"

"My daddy's name is Courtney. I am Courtney Junior. I told you I no dude. My man wouldn't lie to me. Whatever, home girl, you better get a life."

I couldn't wait for James to come pick me up. I had been thinking about asking him his age all day. I prayed he wasn't lying to me. The bell rang for us to go home. I was so excited. As I came out of the building, James was right there waiting for me. He gave me a kiss and brought me some balloons that said, "You are special." I never had a guy buy me balloons before. I smiled the whole way home. James made me feel so special. We rode around before I went home. He loved to show me off to the other guys. He wanted the fellas to know I was his girl. I made it home around 4:30 p.m. It was the same time the bus made it to my area to bring us home. James dropped me off at the gate of my house.

"Baby, don't get out without giving me a kiss."

"Boy, this is too close to home to kiss you."

"Oh, you 'shame to kiss your man in front of your home?"

"No, but someone might see me."

"You must have another boyfriend around somewhere looking."

"No, I don't. I'm just respecting my mom."

"Yeah right."

"Baby, no, I don't."

"I'm just talking to you. It's going to get ugly if I find out you hollering at someone else."

"There is no one else, but you, James. Don't think like that."

"Give me my kiss then." I went on and kissed him. He kissed me for at least two minutes.

"What kind of kiss was that?"

"It's called a kiss to remember, baby." I got out the car.

"I love you, Taquasia."

"Okay!"

James didn't lie about that kiss. I thought about it for the rest of the evening. I went to bed with that kiss on my mind. I got up the next morning to get ready for school, and Jaliya called.

"Taquasia, I'm not coming to school today."

"Why, Jaliya?"

"I'm hanging out with my man."

"Go ahead, girl. I'm going on to school."

"When you get in the office, mark me present."

"It's going to look like you're skipping class, then. You shouldn't worry about it if you're not coming."

"You are right. Well, I'll call you, don't call me, okay? I don't want it to seem obvious for any reason. You might call too early. I am going to act like I missed the bus."

"Okay, Jaliya, be safe."

"All right, sis, thanks for being concerned."

"I'm always that. I gotta go, Jaliya. James will be here in a little while to pick me up. I can't be late."

"Okay, love you and talk to you later."

James came to pick me up in a blue BMW. I was so shocked to be riding in a new car.

"Whose car is this, James?"

"Oh, this is my whip. Do you like it?"

"Yes, it is beautiful."

"I'm going to teach you how to drive it."

"When?"

"On your birthday!"

"You don't even know when is my birthday."

"I was just going to ask you that question, Ms. Smarty-Pants. When is your birthday?"

"January 5 is my birthday."

"My birthday is January 18."

"Wow, can't believe that."

"Yeah, sweetie, you see, there is a connection there."

"I guess so, baby."

"We need to ride to the beach on our birthdays. We can even chill at a motel somewhere. Does that sound good?"

"Yes, the beach does, but not the motel."

"Why not the motel? You must think I'm going to hurt you or something?"

"Naw, I was just saying."

"What were you saying, baby?"

"Nothing!"

"You were saying something."

"Don't worry about it."

"Why not?"

"I'll tell you later."

"Tell me now."

"Please change the subject."

"Okay, sweetie, I'm going to let it ride this time."

"Okay!"

We went to eat at McDonalds. I went to school after that. I leaned over and gave James a kiss this time. I didn't want him to have to ask me.

"Awww, baby, you remember the routine."

"Yes, sweetie, talk to you later."

"Love you, Taquasia."

"Okay!"

"Hell naw, I said 'I love you' twice. You said okay."

"What am I supposed to say?"

"I love you too, babe."

"I'll tell you later."

"Whatever, man, go get your education."

I walked toward the school, and the students started talking about my man's car.

Everyone said he was a drug dealer. I wasn't hearing any of that. I was happy to be with a nice fella like James. On the other hand, I hope my best friend was safe with her new friend. I went on to class. I couldn't stop thinking about James. At lunch they always played music for us to listen. They played Michael Starling, Lovers and Friends. Almost every girl in the cafeteria started crying. We thought about our boyfriends. It sounds strange, huh? But it happened.

When lunch was over, the boys in my class asked, "Why do girls do that every day?"

I told them, "It's called love."

They said, "Yah'll just plain crazy.

I said, "Whatever."

I started doing my work and couldn't wait for the day to be over. On the way to my next class, I ran into Tay.

"Girl, where have you and Jaliya been?"

"We have been at school."

"I haven't been seeing you all."

"I have been getting dropped off by my boyfriend."

"Who is your boyfriend?"

"His name is James."

"Girl, you've been leaving me out on this one."

"Naw, I haven't, I just haven't been seeing you."

"You have been seeing me all before. Why don't you come outside anymore?"

"I don't feel like it. I just am chilling."

"Okay, seems like you're acting funny now since you got you a boyfriend."

"That's how you feel, I am still the same."

"Whatever, dog, just remember that."

"Child, please, sounds like a hater move there."

"I do not hate on you."

"Enjoy yourself. I will talk to you when you feel like you need a friend."

I walked off and went on to class. A new girl started at our school today. All the boys at school tried to talk to her. They made a bet on her that they could talk to her. She was real ghetto and didn't mind speaking her mind. Her name was Cherry.

Cherry let the whole class know if a dude ain't got no money, she don't want him. The boys told Cherry we were just alike. I had never talked to a boy in my class before. No matter how many times they tried. James was my first boyfriend ever. I didn't think I could talk to no one else. Some girls in my class said, "You need two boyfriends." I thought I only needed one. Cherry even said, "You need two boyfriends, so you won't get played by nobody." She said, "It's better you play a man than let a man play you." I thought to myself, *What if she's telling the truth? I just have to wait and see.*

School was out, and my man was waiting for me. I got into the car.

"Hi, baby, I missed you."

"I missed you too, boo."

"What did you learn today?"

"The same thing I learned yesterday. We studied for a test tomorrow."

"Okay," he said, smiling. "I am proud of you for listening in school."

"James, when are you going to school?"

"I'm suspended for fighting."

"Why were you fighting?"

"A dude tried me and thought I wasn't going to do anything. I had to beat him down."

"Okay, so my man is a G?"

"You know it, I'm straight gangster."

"Where are we riding today?"

"Out by Mom's today. I got to handle some business out there."

"Okay!"

"You ready to go home?"

"No, I'm going with you."

"All right, I want you to stay in the car when I get out there."

"I hear you, sweetie."

Chapter 3

A Hater Move

We pulled up at Mom's Café; there were many guys out there. I never had been around so many men in life. There were ugly men, cute men, skinny men, and fat men. They all were up there gambling, loitering, or selling drugs. James started shooting dice. I sat in the car for a good thirty minutes before he came to check on me. It dawned on me that all the guys were men. They were much taller than the boys at my school. *Maybe Courtney Junior was right. Could James be a man and lying about his age? How would I ever find out the truth?* I couldn't really talk to anybody. I wished he came on before the bus made it to my house.

Tay called my mom as soon as she got home and told her that I liked a boy named James.

"Mrs. Carmen, Taquasia and Jaliya have been skipping school with a boy named James."

"Are you sure?"

"Yes, ma'am. James is Taquasia's new boyfriend."

"I don't allow her to date anybody."

"Who is your boyfriend, Tay?"

"I don't have one."

"You are telling on Taquasia and Jaliya. You're in the same boat too. All of you all are friends."

"I was just telling you so that you will know. I don't want anything to happen to her. The children at school say, 'James is a grown man.' They also say, 'James is a drug dealer.'"

"I will take care of Taquasia when she gets home. Thanks for the information, Tay."

"You are welcome, Mrs. Carmen."

James took me home an hour later. On the way home, he said, "Taquasia, I am so sorry. I didn't mean to take so long. It's just gambling takes a while."

"Why would you start gambling when you know I had to be home at a certain time?"

"I wasn't thinking, baby."

"Wow, how could you not think?"

"My mind was in a zone, baby."

"I hope I don't get in trouble, Mr. Zone."

"If you do, then I'll take up the slack."

"Whatever, man, you are going to run far away."

"Seriously, boo! I love you, and you are mine forever."

I started smiling. He reached over and hugged me.

"Baby, you make me smile when I am down."

"Is that a good thing or what?"

"That's a good thing, sugar."

I finally made it home.

"James, did you win the dice game?"

"No, not this time."

"You will know when I do."

"How will I know?"

"I am going to bring you the money. For real, baby!"

"You be playing, babe."

"Sweetheart, I'm going to see you later. I love you, Taquasia."

"Love you too, James."

"See you in the morning, sweetie." He was smiling. Boy, James really meant a lot to me. I wondered, *Does he really love me like he said*?

I walked in the house. I got slapped across the face.

"Where have you been?"

"School, mother!"

"You have not been to school this late. Where have you been, and I want to know now?"

"I had to catch the MTA bus home."

"Why the hell you had to ride the MTA bus home?"

"I missed the school bus. I got out of class late."

"Girl, let's play strip."

"Mom, please, no."

"Yes, take your clothes off, and bring me that belt. Tay already told me you've been skipping school with James."

"Mom, she is lying to you."

"That's your best friend. She wouldn't lie on you like that."

"Yes, she would, Mom."

"She is mad at me because I haven't been talking to her."

"You are going to get your butt back in church. We are going to start back on Sunday. You are not going to get out of hand. I will break your neck if you try me like that. We might have a lot. You don't know what all I go through to make ends meet. I love all my children, and I will be damned if anyone of you all disrespects me. I'm going to call the school tomorrow and see if you have been going. You better pray your ass off you have perfect attendance."

"I don't have to pray because I have been going."

"I heard Jaliya been skipping school too."

"No, ma'am, I'm telling you Tay have hated on everyone."

"You can put your clothes on. I'm going to let you slide this time."

I was so happy. After putting my clothes on, I called Jaliya.

"Girl, guess what Tay told my mom."

"What, girl?"

"She said you and I've been skipping school with James."

"Why that chick lied on me like that?"

"I don't know, girl. She is about crazy."

"I'm going to kick her tail when I get to school."

"Taquasia, I got your back."

"You don't have to worry about that, chick. I'm going to step to her myself."

"I am going to be right there, chick."

"All right, sis! Jaliya, I hope my world don't turn around and slap me in the face."

"It won't, sis! I'm going to let you meet James."

"Okay, sis! I want you to meet my friend also."

"All right!"

"I'll talk to you tomorrow, Jaliya."

"Okay, sis!"

Chapter 4

Showing Some Love

James picked me up from the bus stop. Tay saw me and rolled her eyes. I really didn't care. I was going to handle her when I got to school. We went riding around town before school again.

"Baby, where are we going?"

"We are going to run in the flea market before you go to school. I seen some shoes I want to get you."

"What kind?"

"I saw some Ewings that match your outfit this morning."

"Okay!"

We pulled up to the flea market. James came and opened my side of the car door. We walked into the flea market holding hands. I really didn't want no shoes after I saw all that jewelry. I stopped by the jewelry booth.

"Baby, I like these bangles."

"How many you want?"

"How many can you afford to get?"

"That's not what I asked you."

"Well, I want about twelve bracelets."

"Okay, just tell the lady how many you want."

"Ma'am, can I have twelve of your small bangles?"

"Let me see your arm, young lady."

I gave the woman my arm. She had to see what size fit my arm. The woman gave me two extra ones. James paid the lady, and we kept walking.

"Thank you, babe!"

"You're welcome!"

We made it to the booth with all the high-top shoes. The man had every kind of Ewing there was.

"Tell the man your size."

"I wear a 6 1/2 in shoes."

James bought me a pair of orange, blue, and white ones. They were so pretty. We left the flea market. He took me to McDonalds, then to school.

"Thanks again, James. I really appreciate it."

"You're welcome anytime. I told you I want you to be dressed fresh every day. You can take those Pro Wings off. Put on your new shoes. Leave the old ones in the car and take them out after school."

"Okay!"

"Put your bangles on. Give your man a kiss."

We smacked each others' lips, and I got out the car.

"I love you, James."

"Love you too, sweetie!" He drove off.

I knew I was prettier than ever now. I love jewelry; it brings out my skin's complexion. I went in school with my breakfast. I looked for my best friend Jaliya. I saw her sitting in the cafeteria.

"What's up, homey?"

"I brought breakfast for us."

"Thanks, girl, this breakfast isn't about nothing this morning."

"I saw Tay at the bus stop."

"Did you say anything to her?"

"No, James pulled up in his car. I got in with him. Let's eat, then go find her."

"Cool, sis!"

"Look, dog, we don't have to find her. She is going to the breakfast line now. We will front her on the way to class."

"Yeah!"

My skin was boiling. I was getting madder and madder by the minute. The bell rang for us to go to class. I got up before Jaliya.

"Taquasia, are you all right?"

"Come on! I feel like popping off on her."

"Do what you do."

Tay took a long time to come out the cafeteria.

"Taquasia, you don't need to fight her now. There are too many people watching. Wait until the crowd go to class. You will see her in the hallways."

"Okay!"

I went on to my first-period class. "Jaliya, I'll holler at you later."

"Okay!"

I went in Mrs. Ledo's class. Everyone was excited about all the jewelry I had on.

"Dang, Taquasia, looks like life is treating you lovely."

"You know it. I just got a hater on my team. She got to go though."

One of my classmates said, "Keep females out of your business, and you will make it."

"Thanks for the advice."

I finished up my assignment. Mrs. Ledo wanted me to go make copies of her test. I left her class to make copies. As I was walking through the hall, a dude tried to talk to me. He walked me to the copier room.

"Baby, what's up?"

"Nothing!"

"Who is your boyfriend?"

"James Lyons!"

"That's a grown man. I thought you were going to say someone from school. Dang, li'l mama! Why you don't have a school man?"

"He is in school."

"Naw, shawty, he is a drug dealer."

"Whatever, man!"

He walked off. I was so glad. He was really ticking me off. I took my teacher back her tests.

"Thank you, Taquasia!"

"You are welcome, Mrs. Ledo."

Cherry came to class late.

"What's up, Taquasia? You're bling-blinging over there. When did you get those bangles?"

"This morning!"

"Your man must bought them for you?"

"Yeah, chick!"

"Girl, you better keep him. It feels good to have a man that spoils you, huh?"

"Yeah!"

"Why are you late, chick?"

"I woke up late. My man's clock didn't alarm on time."

"You stay with your boyfriend?"

"No, he stays with me."

"Where do you stay?"

"I live with my mom. She doesn't care though. My mom lets us have sex and all."

"What! That's so disrespectful!"

"How is it disrespectful when she don't care?"

"Dang!"

The bell rang. It was time for our next class. I saw Tay coming up the hall. I dropped my books and punched her in the face. We fought as if we were never friends. With every punch I threw, I asked her, "Why you lied to my mother?" She never responded. We kept fighting. The crowd got bigger and bigger. They pushed Tay and me, trying to see the fight. Finally someone snatched us apart. We were sent to the office. The office called our house. Neither of our parents was home. The principal asked, "Why were you girls fighting?"

"Taquasia was mad because her man tried to talk to me."

"Girl, quit lying. My man would never try to talk to you. Sir, she called my mom, lying, yesterday. She told my mom I've been skipping school. She tried to make me get a whipping."

"Well, do you skip school?"

"No, sir!"

"I hope the fighting is over."

The principal sent us to ISS. That was cool with me. I didn't want to go home.

ISS was fun. We had a lot of fun people in class. All of the class clowns were in there. The ISS teacher wanted to know why we were fighting. We had to explain everything to her. It was real stupid. It could have been avoided. I just had to let her know not to try me like that ever again. My best friend Jaliya came to check on me. The teacher wouldn't let us talk though. The ISS lady said, "Come straight to ISS every morning for three days. Do not miss any days or be tardy. If you do, I will add an extra day to your in-school suspension."

We sat there for the rest of the day. I was so happy when the bell rang to go home. I went out in the front to wait on my man. He never came. *Where could he be?* The school buses have left already. I didn't have enough money to catch the Metro bus. I went back in the school to call home. My mom didn't answer the phone. I called James's house; he wasn't there.

My best bet was to start walking home. I walked all the way home. I made it there around 6:00 p.m. My mom was worried.

"Where have you been, Taquasia?"

"I got bus left. I tried to call you, Mom, to tell you."

"I went grocery shopping. I'm going to give you more numbers in case of emergency."

"Yes, ma'am!"

James didn't call or pick me up anymore for a while. I thought I would never see him again. I never took naps. I cried myself to sleep on this incident. The more I thought about him, the more he never came back. I didn't know if he got locked up or what. I started to get over him. I had to get use to riding the bus all over again.

Chapter 5

The Big Fight

I saw James a week before my birthday. My mom sent me to the store to purchase some bread. I walked straight pass him when I saw him.

"Dang, li'l mama, you don't see me."

I kept walking. He came in the store behind me.

"Taquasia, you are going to walk straight pass me like that?"

"What's up, James?"

"I can't believe this shit here."

"James, I'm not stun you anymore. You haven't called me or anything. I'm not going to run behind you."

"Listen, baby, you haven't called me either."

"Yes, I have."

"Taquasia, why you got to lie to daddy?"

"Boy, I'm not lying to no one. You need to stop your mess talking about daddy. You don't take care of me."

"I love you, and I show you in so many ways."

"All right, whatever!"

"I haven't seen any number on my caller ID."

"You haven't been home to see it."

"I know you aren't talking to daddy like that."

"Boy, stop! You're killing me with this daddy mess."

"Baby, you're lying to daddy. I don't like you lying to me out of all people. Daddy will spank you if you keep on lying to me."

"Whatever, dude! Let me straighten you now. I don't have a daddy. I don't have a father either, so get it right. I really don't have to listen to no man at all. My father is dead. You can never take his place because he is six feet under."

"I know you aren't back talking me, girl."

"What do you mean back talking you? You're not grown. At least that is what you tell me. Why don't you get out my face, dog?"

James rushed out the store with anger. I really didn't care. I paid for the bread and walked out the store. James grabbed my left arm.

"Are you done being sassy now?"

"Man, leave me alone and get out my face."

"I see you have got grown now. I'm going to have to tighten your pants up."

"Whatever, dude! I'm not worried about you anymore."

The dudes around the store said, "Man, I know you're not letting her back talk you like that."

"She straight I got her."

"Got who, James?"

I looked into James's eyes. His eyes were bloodshot red. He was mad enough to beat me up probably. I removed his hand from around my wrist. I went back into the store to purchase some arrow heads. I bought every flavor since they were only fifteen cents a piece. I went back out the store. I felt a hard slap across my face. The slap was so hard that the bread hit the ground. I had to hold on to the pole so I wouldn't fall. My head was spinning around and around. All I could say was, "Oh my god. I know you didn't slap me." I ran up to him after getting my vision back. He knocked me down to the ground next to the bread. "Girl, don't ever try that shit again. You never back talk me. Do you understand me?" I got up off the ground with embarrassment. I got my mom's bread and started walking home. I could hear the dudes from the store, saying, "Good job, dog. You don't ever let no female talk to you any kind of way."

I kept walking onto my house. In my head, I couldn't believe I just got punked in front of all them people like that. *He better be glad I had to take this bread home to my mom. I would have tried to get him back. I probably still will.*

I made it to the house. My little sister Tanzia said, "Taquasia, what happened to your face?"

"I don't know. What does it look like?"

"It is swollen."

"What?"

I placed the bread in the kitchen and went to the bathroom. I looked in the mirror. My face had swollen up on one side. I really got pissed off. There wasn't anything I could do about it. I couldn't tell anyone but my best friend Jaliya. We probably could jump him or something. He was built, and we probably couldn't beat him. I was not going to worry about it. I went back into the kitchen to place ice on my face. My mom said, "What happened to your face?" I told her something stung me on my way to the store, and I was scratching it because it was itching. She took a look at it and said, "Place the ice on there. I will check it out when the swelling goes down."

"Okay."

Later on that day, James called to apologize.

"Hello, may speak to Taquasia?"

"Hold on. Taquasia, come get the telephone."

"Who is it, Ta'Shontie?"

"I don't know, it's a man."

"Who, a man calling for me?"

"Yes!"

"Hang up, he must have the wrong number." *Click!*

"I hung up the phone, Taquasia."

"Okay!"

The phone began to ring again. Ta'Shontie answered the phone.

"Taquasia, he said come get the phone."

"Tell him he got the wrong number, and hang the phone up."

"She said you must have the wrong number."

"Tell her, 'This is James, get the phone.'"

"Taquasia, he said, 'This James.'"

"Tell him I don't want to talk to him. Just hang up the phone."

"Okay, sis!"

James called back once more. I picked the phone up and hung it back up.

"Who was that, Taquasia?"

"Somebody had the wrong number, Mom."

"Mommy, somebody named James keep playing on the phone for Taquasia."

"Girl, shut up," I told her.

"Okay! Who you said, Ta'Shontie?"

"A boy named James." She ran off and started playing.

"Taquasia, why is James playing on my phone?"

"I don't know. He probably was looking for Dre or something."

"Have you been talking to Dre lately?"

"No, ma'am."

"He isn't looking for Dre. Everybody knows Dre is locked up."

"I didn't know that."

"How you didn't know? He is your best friend. You guys usually talk every day."

"We haven't been talking lately. How long has he been locked up, Mom? He is going to kill me for not writing him."

"He has been locked up going over a month now."

"Wow! Mom, can you buy me some stamps to write him."

"Yes!"

"Can you find his address?"

"You can get it from his grandma."

"Okay!"

"He also was trying to call from the Dade County jail. Did you accept his call?"

"Yes, but he never called back anymore."

"Now back to this James situation. He can't be looking for Dre now, could he?"

"Well, if he doesn't know he's locked up, he would be."

"It's more to it than that."

"No, it isn't, Mom."

"You're going to make me nut up on James and you. Don't try to make me out of a fool. You better believe you're going to hate it. Stop trying to blame everything on Dre. Be honest with yourself."

"Yes, ma'am. If James is calling, he might be checking to see if I heard from Dre."

"All right, when he calls back, answer the phone, then. I want to see what you guys are talking about."

"Yes, ma'am!" *I hope he doesn't call back.*

"James's name has been popping up a lot lately. I need to get to the bottom of this."

"I don't know why, Mom. He is just cool with everybody."

"Everybody like whom!"

"He is cool with everybody throughout town. He is a popular guy."

"Well, if he's so popular, I could ask questions about him. Everyone should know who I'm talking about. I'll see! You know I will ask questions now."

"I know, Mom."

"Just don't let your lies catch up with you. Your ass belongs to me if you do."

"Yes, ma'am."

"How old is James?"

"He said he was eighteen years old."

"What is his last name?"

"I don't know."

"How you don't know?"

"I never asked him. Besides, that's Dre's home boy, not mine."

"You know his last name. You don't want me to find out. You're trying to keep it a secret. I will find out everything I need to know."

"I know, Mom. I'm not keeping any secrets." In my mind, I wished the conversation would end. It only got worse.

A knock came at the door. I was glad so she could get off the subject.

"Hello, James, we were just discussing you."

"Yeah!" He was grilling hard.

"Come in, James, join our conversation. Have a seat."

I was so nervous. This boy had a lot of nerves to come to my house like this. My heart dropped to my stomach. I went in my room as James was sitting down on the couch.

"Taquasia, come here. Let's finish our discussion."

My head began to hurt real badly. I didn't know what to do or say. It's as if my brain was out of words.

"How have you been doing, James?"

"I'm straight, Mrs. Carmen. How have you been, Mrs. Carmen?"

"Great! I feel even better since you're here."

I sat on the love seat by myself.

"Come sit next to James, Taquasia."

"I don't want to sit next to him, Mom. I don't feel comfortable doing that."

"Girl, come sit down. I'm not going to bite you."

My mom sat in the lazy boy chair right in front of us. "Now I want to get to the bottom of this."

"What's this about, Mrs. Carmen?"

"I want to know what is going on with you and my daughter. The rumor is that Taquasia has been skipping school with you."

"She knows I don't play that skipping school shit. I am a Christian, and I don't suppose to be cursing."

"You all are making me go off the wall. What is going on?"

"Well, Mrs. Carmen, I am going to be honest with you. I do like your daughter. I will never ask or make her skip school. She has been going to school every day. If I find out she isn't, I will beat her for you."

"No, you won't put your hands on my child. You could let me know though."

This dude was about crazy. My mom was about crazy too. I didn't know why she let this dude in our house. He was starting to make me nervous.

"James, what brought you this way?"

"I wanted to get your permission on dating your daughter."

"My daughter is not allowed to date anyone. She is only in the eighth grade. What grade are you in?"

"I am in the twelfth grade."

"You are a big twelfth grader. You must stayed back about three years?"

"No, ma'am." He was smiling.

"Taquasia, do you like James?"

"No, ma'am!"

"You don't like me, Taquasia?"

"No, James, I don't."

"You can tell your mom the truth, sweetie."

"No, boy, you have gone crazy. I said I don't like you. Wow! What part of do not you don't understand?"

"I really needed to talk to your daughter. That's another reason I came over here."

"What is the other reason, James?"

"She knows, ask her."

I started breathing hard. I just wanted to fake an asthma attack.

"What is he talking about, Taquasia?"

"I don't know, Mom."

"What are you talking about, Mr. James? I need to know too."

"You know what's going on between us."

"Boy, stop playing and get a life."

"What the fuck is going on between you two? You better not have had sex with this boy."

"No, ma'am."

"What is it? Why is it so hard to answer the question then?"

"I told you all, nothing is going on between us. Yeah, you tried to talk to me or whatever. I do not like you. It's just plain and simple." I got up to go in my room.

"Come back here and sit down. The conversation isn't over until I said it's over."

"That's right!" he said, smiling. "See, Mrs. Carmen? I really like your daughter a lot."

"How do you know you like my daughter?"

"I know because she makes me smile. I have her in my thoughts and my dreams. She means the world to me. I promise you, I won't hurt her either."

"The thing is, Taquasia is thirteen years old."

"She will be fourteen tomorrow."

"You are way too old for her."

"I really like her a lot though."

"If you really like her, you would wait until she is grown. I can't let you ruin her life."

"What do you mean 'ruin her life'? I can make it better for you and her."

"How can you do that? I can get a job and work. I can help you pay bills."

"You must think you moving in?"

"No, ma'am. I just want to help out."

"How old are you, James?"

"I'm eighteen years old."

"What school do you attend?"

"I go to Homestead Senior High School. I'm really a senior this year. I want you to come to my graduation."

"All right, I will be there."

"I know your daughter is young. I just want to be there for her. I will support her in school. I promise not to cheat on her for nobody. I won't treat her wrong at all."

"You look like a grown man. You sure you aren't a grown acting like a child?"

"No, ma'am!" he said, smiling.

"Where do you work?"

"I'm planning on getting a job soon. I have been putting in applications at different places. I just have to make sure it fits my school schedule."

"What movie is that on television?"

"That's *New Jack City* coming on."

"Oh yeah, I wanted to see that. *New Jack City* just came out."

"Yeah, it did."

"You can watch it with us."

I got up and went to my room. I stayed in my room until the movie was over. I was scared because James was brave enough to come to my house. What else could he have up his sleeve? He asked my mom permission to date me. He wasn't even scared of my mom. After the movie, James got up to leave.

"Mrs. Carmen, thanks for letting me watch the movie."

"You're welcome!"

"Is it all right if I call Taquasia sometimes?"

"Only if you promise to just call her, I'm not giving you permission to date her."

"Yes, ma'am! Tell Taquasia I'll talk to her tomorrow."

"All right, have a good evening."

"Taquasia, come here now."

I walked into the living room where my mom was. Here comes the drama now. I didn't even know what to tell her. I couldn't tell her I lied the whole time. Should I tell her the truth? She might beat the breaks off me then. I really didn't know what to say. I knew I hated that I lied to her. I just didn't want to get in trouble. Now I had to look at her in her face.

"Baby, why you lied to me?"

"I don't know, Mom. I was scared you were going to beat me or something."

"Have you ever skipped school with him?"

"No, ma'am!"

"Are you lying about that too?"

"No, ma'am! He just has been trying to talk to me, that is all."

"He ever asked you to skip school?"

"No, ma'am."

"Don't be a fool for nobody. Do you understand? A lot of guys are going to try and talk to you. You don't ever let them get your goodies. That's all most guys want from a female."

"Yes, ma'am!"

"You don't need any babies. You are too young for that. Try to finish school before you let anyone break your virginity. You will feel better about yourself. Go make yourself a sandwich now and go to sleep. You need all the rest you can get for school tomorrow."

"Okay, Mom!"

Chapter 6

Happy Birthday

I woke this morning bright and early. I was excited that it was my birthday. I got ready for school. I left early to catch the bus. My shirt was purple and white. I wore some see-through white tights to match my shirt. I had some white heels on to match my outfit. I knew I was pretty for my birthday. I had my hair in a mushroom. James drove up to the bus stop. He was driving his purple Lei Vaton Cadillac. He had a car full of balloons in the backseat. I didn't want to ride to school with James that morning. I wanted to hang out with my best friend today.

"Baby, get in the car."

"I want to ride the bus today."

"I want to take you to breakfast for your birthday."

"I really want to ride the bus."

"Well, I want you to ride with me."

"Okay, but I want to ride the bus home."

"Girl, get in the car before someone sees you."

I got in the car. I really wanted to chill with my best friend. I hadn't been spending much time with her on the bus.

James took me to Shoney's Restaurant. It was just like Denny's, but fancier. We ate a big breakfast. After leaving Shoney's, we went to a big brick house.

"James, whose house is this?"

"My sister's house, you can get out."

"Naw, I might be late for school."

"Man, get out the car."

I got out the car. James unlocked the door with a key. He acted as if it was his house. He didn't knock or anything.

"Have a seat, baby."

I sat down on the couch. He walked into a room in the back. He came back into the living room about three minutes later. Maybe he went to take a bowel movement or something. He put the radio on. It wasn't anything playing he wanted to hear. He put on the CD player. Gerald Levert started singing "Baby Hold On to Me." He came and sat beside me.

"Happy birthday, baby! I want this to be a birthday you won't ever forget."

He leaned over and pop-kissed me. He got up and went to the car. He came back in the house with five balloons. "Baby, these are for you." James started the CD back over. He put it on Repeat. I guess that's his favorite song.

James stood in front of me and started singing, "Baby, hold on to me." It was so cute. He grabbed my hands to pull me from the couch. We started slow-dancing in the living room. After the song went off, we walked into the back into another room.

"You could have a seat on the bed."

"All right!"

I wondered what this dude got up his sleeves. James started talking.

"Taquasia, you know I really love you. I want to spend your birthday with you. This is your first birthday with me. I just want it to be special. You are my baby now. I don't want you to go to school today. I will have you home on time. I promise you, sweetie! Are you happy to be with me?"

"Yes, baby!"

He went into the drawer and pulled out a box.

"I have something special for you." He gave me the box. It was a 24k gold nameplate necklace. I smiled so hard. I never had a 24k gold necklace before.

I wanted to still go to school. I knew the school would announce my birthday all day. They would also give me a gift. I was an office aid at school. I loved my school. I didn't want my mom to find out I missed school. I couldn't break her heart like that.

"James, I hope my mom doesn't find out I missed school with you."

"She won't, who will tell her? You damn sho aren't going to tell her. You denied me to her. You will die with this secret. I know you will."

I laughed! James leaned over and kissed me. I kissed him back. He pressed his lips against mine. It wasn't a pop kiss. It was more like a pressure kiss.

"We are going to stay at my sister's house until it's time for my sister to get off work."

"Okay, what if your sister comes home early?"

"She won't say anything. She is down-to-earth. Baby, since it's early in the morning, we can go back to sleep."

We took our shoes off and climbed farther in the bed. "Taquasia, you can lay on my arms, sweetie." I lay in the center of his arm. He placed his other arm around me too. "Baby girl, I've been waiting to lie next to you for a long time now. I didn't know it would be your birthday when it happened. I wanted to tell you sorry about what I did at the store. It won't happen again."

"You promise?"

"I promise on everything I love."

"Okay!"

"Look at me, baby, while I talk to you. You are going to be my wife one day."

I listened to everything he said. He reached over and kissed me again. This time, the kissing didn't stop. He put his tongue in my mouth. I didn't know what he was doing. He kissed me around my neck. He stopped and said, "Suck on my tongue this time. I need you to tongue-kiss me back."

I really didn't know what tongue kissing was. I didn't know anything about tongue kissing. I tried it though. I felt a sharp feeling going through my body. Could that be electricity or something? It went from my chest to my stomach. It felt like butterflies flying around in me. I never felt like this before. What was James trying to do to me? James kissed my neck again. This time, he was kissing and sucking my neck at the same time. It felt good whatever he was trying to do. While sucking on my neck, he was unbuttoning my shirt. I stopped his hands. "What are you doing, sweetie?"

"I just wanted to see what your body looked like."

"I don't like to show my body to anyone."

"Baby, I'm not just anyone. I'm your man."

I hope this boy don't think he is going to break my virginity. He is going to get his feelings hurt if he does try it.

"You don't like me sucking on your neck?"

"Yeah! What you got up your sleeve?"

"Nothing, baby, just relax."

"You must like kissing my neck?"

"Hell yeah, I like it. Are you a virgin, baby?"

"Yes, sweetheart! I'm going to stay a virgin until I get married."

"Yeah!" he said, smiling. "Why you want to stay a virgin until you're married? What if I'm going to be your husband?"

"Well, we will have to wait and see."

"I told you I am going to be your husband. I'm trying to show you in so many ways."

He started sucking on my neck again. This time, I started to feel the sensation. It felt as if my body was getting heated. I didn't know what he was feeling like at that moment. I was too scared to ask. Maybe this was what Cherry was talking about in school. He stepped down to the floor. He removed his shirt. He was a dark chocolate. James had a muscular chest. He also had a six-pack stomach. I really knew this was a moment I wouldn't ever forget. He undressed all the way down to his boxers. James lay on top of me. He kissed my body from my head to stomach. I was in a daze, boy. Maybe he won't go any further than this kissing scheme. James started pulling my tights down.

"Baby, what are you doing?"

"Just relax. I'm not going to hurt you."

He placed his penis through his boxer. His penis was big.

"What are you going to do with that?" James started smiling.

"Just chill out, sweetie!"

"I can't until you tell me what you planning on doing with your penis."

"Ha-ha! Nothing, man, just chill out. You are messing up my concentration."

His sister came home. She cut the music off. He jumped up so fast. James rushed and put his clothes on. I had to put my clothes on. We both sat up on the bed. Laura entered the room.

"Why you have the music so loud?"

"Man, I don't know."

"How you doing, young lady?"

"Fine, and you?"

"Don't let my brother mess your life up. You better go to school."

"Yes, ma'am."

"Why you home so early, sis?"

"I forgot my lunch. I also have to drop my car off to the shop. I need you to follow me to the shop and take me to work."

"Okay!"

"You ready now?"

"Yes!"

"Come, Taquasia, let's go and handle this business for my sister."

We got into the car and left. Laura relieved me by coming home. We were gone for at least an hour. We went by James's mother's house. He went to get some changing clothes. We headed back to his sister's house.

Chapter 7

Entering Womanhood

We made it back to James's sister's house. He put the music back on. We went back into the room. James took my tights off. "Damn, baby, you look good." He loosened my shirt and took my bra off. I was straight naked. I was embarrassed. No one besides my mother had ever seen me naked. He kept staring at my body. "Baby, you look good as hell." I started blushing. "I am serious, sugar." He leaned over and kissed my breast. I didn't know what to do. He kept saying my body looked good as hell. I had heard my mother having sex before. I had never seen it. What was I supposed to do?

James kept sucking on my neck. He licked me from my head to my navel. He moved back up slowly. I felt as if I was in wonderland. Whatever he was doing, it felt good. He pressed his penis against my vagina. He started shaking his penis on top of my vagina. Next, he tried placing his penis head to my vaginal hole. My baby tried to enter his penis in. It still wouldn't go in.

"James, maybe now isn't the right time."

"I got it, sweetie."

He moved his body back and forth, back and forth. He tried putting his penis in my vagina again. He moved back and forth, back and forth. It felt as if he was ripping my skin.

"Uh! Uh! Are you trying to break my vagina?"

"No, sweetie, I'm trying to make it feel good."

"Well, it hurts. It doesn't feel good."

"Baby, just relax and let daddy take care of you."

I lay there while he pressed his way in.

"James, you're hurting me!" I screamed real loud as he pushed all the way in my vagina. "Ouch!" He was in now. James moved in and out of me. I tried to move up the wall to get away. I crawled to the wall backward. He moved up along with me. I was in a Spider Man position, how Spider Man crawls up the wall backward to get away from danger.

I screamed as loud as the radio. James was moaning and talking.

"Is this my coochie, baby?" I didn't say anything. I laughed!

"Whose coochie this is, baby?"

"Mine!"

He started stroking his penis deeper in me. I started screaming louder and louder.

"Whose coochie this is, baby?"

"Mine, damn it!" He stroked even harder. The pain became more unbearable. I tried to get up from under him. His body was too heavy.

"All you got to do, Taquasia, is answer the question."

"What question?"

"Whose coochie this is?"

"I answered the question many times."

"Wrong answer! Is this my coochie from now on?"

"James, it's yours if you want it to be yours."

"Damn, baby, why do you want to make things so difficult?"

We had sex from 9:00 a.m. until 11:00 a.m. My body was so tired. My vagina was hurting.

"James, you tried to kill my vagina."

"Ha-ha! It was good though. You didn't like it?"

"Man, having sex hurts."

"It won't hurt as bad next time."

"It won't be a next time."

"Whatever! Come on, let's shower up."

As I was getting out the bed, blood was running down my legs. I almost passed out.

"James, you knocked my period on?"

"No, I didn't, I bust your cherry." He was smiling.

"You like that, huh?"

"Yeah, you my lady now."

"Okay, remember what you just said."

He kissed my forehead. We entered the shower together. James put the soap on the rag and bathed my body all over.

I never had this happened to me before. I had shivers all over my body. James picked me up and propped my body up against the wall. I wrapped my legs around him so I wouldn't fall. He placed his penis inside my vagina again. He started stroking my body while I was propped against the wall. The water ran all over our bodies. It felt better having sex in the shower than on the bed. I felt myself moving back and forth with the motion. It felt good for the moment until James made a loud noise.

"Uh-uh!"

"Man, what was all that?"

"I got me a nut."

"What?"

"You will get one soon. Just keep on dealing with me."

"Whatever, James!" I smiled.

James walked backed into the bedroom to change the sheets on the bed. It's like from that moment on I grew attached to him. We lay down beside each other in the bed.

"James, I can't believe I just had sex."

"Why not? This will be a day you will always remember."

"I believe that too."

"I love you, James."

"I love you too, baby."

"I thought we were supposed to go to South Beach for my birthday? You said you were going to show me how to drive today."

"I am, baby. We just won't be able to go to South Beach today. We ran out of time."

Both of us fell to sleep in each other's arms. We woke around 3:00 p.m. My tights were bloody on one side. I was so embarrassed. I was ready to go home and change clothes. I went to the bathroom and put tissue in my panties. We left the house. James took me riding around town. He tried to let me drive down Redland Road. I was nervous. I tried driving with two feet. He placed one of his hands on the steering wheel. He coached me to stay in my lane. I was happy to be learning how to drive. This really was a birthday to remember.

"Pull over slowly, baby." We changed seats. As we changed seats, one of my cousins drove by and saw me. I knew she was going to call my mom. School wasn't even out yet. What kind of birthday would this be now?

Chapter 8

Busted in Action

I made it home around 4:30 p.m. My mother wasn't home yet. My cousin Tisha had called when I looked at the caller ID. I rushed and took a bath. I changed my clothes. I stuffed the dirty ones in the bottom of the clothes hamper. My cousin called again. She just wanted to snitch on me. I hadn't ever done anything to her. Tisha left my mother a voice mail. I erased it. The school called to let my mother know I missed school. I was so glad I caught that call. I called my best friend Jaliya to tell her what had happened.

"May I speak to Jaliya?"

"No, she is on punishment."

"What? What she did?"

"She skipped school today. Did you skip school with her?"

"No, ma'am!"

"Well, she did, and her ass belongs to me."

"Is she home now?"

"Yeah!"

"May I please talk to her for one minute?"

"All right, one minute!"

"Jaliya, please sneak and call me before the night is over with."

"Okay! Girl, let me gone and take this beating."

"I'm probably going to get one too."

"All right, chick!"

"Love you, sis!"

"Love you too."

My mother walked in the door with my little brother. I was so scared. I didn't know if I should make something up or tell the truth.

"Happy birthday, Taquasia!"

"Thanks, Mom!"

"Happy birthday, Taquasia! I love you too, sister!"

"Thanks!"

"Mom, can I talk to you alone?"

"Go ahead, sweetie, say what you got to say."

"Mother, can I speak to you without Tonio around?"

"Yes, give me a few minutes."

"Okay!"

My cousin called again.

"Where's Carmen at? She is 'sleep right now? Wake her up, grown ass. I know you didn't tell her I saw you with that grown man. I am going to tell her when she wakes up. You better and tell her to call me."

"Okay! If she doesn't call me, I will be over there."

"Yes, ma'am!" I felt like running away at that moment. I didn't know where to go. I didn't know why I skipped school with James. I knew I would regret it afterward. The fun only lasted a little while.

The phone started ringing again with a private number.

"Hello! Is Carmen there?"

"She is asleep. May I ask who is calling?"

"Patricia!"

"I will tell her you called." I thought about it. Patricia never called my house before. That's got to be my cousin Tisha. She was trying to play as if I'm stupid. I wanted to tell my mother first. I didn't want anyone else to tell her.

"Mother, can I please talk to you?"

"Come on and talk to me. What's wrong? What's the rush?"

"Mom, I did something today."

"What did you do, sweetie?"

"I rode home with James after school. I wanted to tell you before someone else told you."

"Why didn't you catch the bus?"

"I don't know."

"I'm going to have another talk with James. You are grounded. No telephone for you. Call James now so I can talk to him."

"Yes, ma'am! Mother, Tisha's seen me also."

"Where she seen you all at?"

"On Redland Road! He was showing me how to drive."

"What is he showing you how to drive for?"

"Today is my birthday, and he promised me he would show me."

The phone was ringing off the hook. Tisha called, and Mom answered the phone.

"What's up, Tisha?"

"I saw your daughter getting out of the car with a grown man."

"What, she claimed she was driving."

"She probably was. It looks like they were switching seats."

"That's probably why she told me then."

"Yeah! She looked me dead in the face. She knew I was going to tell you."

"Thanks, Tisha!"

"You're welcome, Auntie!"

"Taquasia, bring your ass to me now."

I walked into the living room where my mom was at. Mother had a brown extension cord ready to plaster my tail. I only could go ahead and take the whipping. I was wrong for not going to school.

Each time she whipped me, I felt my skin whipping up. I cried so much that my eyes were bloodshot red. I had a headache and only felt like going to sleep.

"Go take a bath now, Taquasia. You better still be a virgin."

"I am."

"You are so sneaky. I am going to have to start walking you to the bus."

"You don't have to do that."

"Yes, I do. You just got grown all of certain." I couldn't say anything. I just looked at my mom in the face. If she only knew what really happened today, Mother probably would kill me.

My mother went to sleep. I sneaked and called James. I explained to him what had happened.

"James, please do not come pick me up from the bus tomorrow. My mom is walking me to the bus."

"Okay, sweetie! That's messed up. I'm going to straighten Tisha when I see her."

"You know her?"

"Yeah! I'm going to get you a beeper. What color do you want?"

"See-through purple."

"I got it baby. I'll talk to you tomorrow."

"How?"

"I'll see you at school."

"Okay!"

"I love you, Taquasia. I hate this has happened to you."

"I love you too. It's okay!"

"No, it isn't. Your mom wasn't supposed to find out so soon."

"She doesn't know we had sex. She just knows we were riding together."

"Okay! Good night, baby!"

"Good night. I am going to miss you."

"You will only miss me for a short period of time. Let's just let things die down some. You hear me, baby?"

"Yes, sweetie!"

"There are other ways to see each other."

"Okay!"

"Talk to you later."

"Okay!"

The next morning came. My mom walked me to the bus stop. Everybody was laughing at me. My mom started praying out loud for everyone. After she prayed, she started singing church music until the bus driver came. My mom told the bus driver, "Don't let her get off the bus until she gets to school."

"All right, Carmen!"

"Thanks!"

I sat down on the bus. I started thinking about James. He had become an important part of me now. Jaliya got on the bus this morning also. We had so much to talk about now.

Jaliya entered the bus. "Girl, what's up?"

"Nothing, I got a beaten yesterday for skipping school."

"Me too, dawg!"

"You got a beaten on your birthday?"

"Yeah, two beatings!"

"What!"

"Dawg, I got my virginity broke yesterday. It felt like James was beating up my vagina. The second beatin' was when my mom found out I was riding with James."

"Girl, naw! I got a beaten for having sex in my mother's house."

"What!" I busted out laughing. "What made you do that?"

"I got my virginity broke yesterday too. It's not like I tried too. It just happened."

"Yeah, I know. The same thing happened here. It's cool though! It's done and over with."

We finally arrived at school.

"Girl, your man is out there waiting for you."

"James said he was going to keep it real with me. I guess he is keeping his promise."

"I'm going to walk over with you, girl."

"That's cool."

I walked to the car, smiling so hard. He got out and gave me a hug.

"I'm really sorry about yesterday. I wanted it to be the best day you ever had."

"Okay!"

"I brought you a beeper from the flea market last night. I will beep you to let you know when I'm thinking about you."

"Okay, that's sweet of you."

"I brought you breakfast also. I'm going to miss you for a little while."

"Me too!"

"Don't cheat on me, baby."

"I won't even think about it at all."

"Damn, this shit is hard. You are about to make me cry, girl. I already cried last night." We hugged as if we were never going to see each other again. We kissed; then the bell rang for us to go to class.

"I love you, James."

"Me too!"

I walked on to class with Jaliya. I had tears in my eyes. "Don't cry, Taquasia. Things are going to get better."

"I know! I just miss him already. I feel like it's going to be a while before I see him again."

"Don't think like that, sis."

I was in class thinking about James. I really couldn't concentrate today. I did my work, but it's hard to stay focused. I went to lunch, and as the slow music played, it made me cry. It was going to be so hard not being with my man. I didn't know how long I could put up with this. I talked to Cherry about what happened. I just needed more advice from another source.

"Cherry, what should I do? My mom found out that I have been hanging out with James. I let him broke my virginity, girl. Now I won't be able to be with him like that because my mom is starting to walk me to the bus stop."

"What, girl, naw! You probably have to call him when you can. I wouldn't worry about it. He isn't going to leave you. He knows he is your first"

"Thanks for the advice, girl."

"You're welcome!"

I went to my locker. We were getting ready to go home. James came out to the school. "Taquasia, I will be at the game room later. Stop by if you can. If you can't, try and call me later."

"Okay! Love you, baby!"

"Love you too!" I ran to the bus. I kind of felt better after seeing him.

At the bus stop, my mother was waiting for me to get off. I was so embarrassed. My classmates were laughing at me. My mom sang gospel songs all the way down the road. We finally made it home.

"Taquasia, I'm going to take you to the doctor."

"For what, Mom!"

"I want to see if you still have your virginity."

"I do!"

"I don't know about that."

"What do you mean?"

"I washed clothes today. I seen your underwear, and they don't look like a period. It looks like cum is in it."

"I don't know what that is."

"You will find out soon enough."

Mother called Martin Luther King Clinic to set me up an appointment. My appointment was set for February 7. Wow! That's a long way away. I didn't care though. My vagina would be back tight by then. Two weeks had passed. James and I beeped each other. We had to sneak and talk on the phone. I hated doing that. The month rolled around fast. I started getting sick for some odd reason. About three weeks later, I started throwing up. Every morning I got up for school, I was sick. I always threw up yellowish acid. It felt as if I stayed hungry.

I called Jaliya to ask her what she think might be going on. She responded, "You might be pregnant, bitch." I told her she was crazy. "Taquasia, listen, you have been doing grown woman things. Anything could have happened. Did he wear a condom?"

"Nope! Hell, naw, dawg!"

"Why you didn't make him wear a condom?"

"I tried! He just didn't use one."

"That's messed up. I hope he didn't give you a disease."

"I hope not either. Momma said she is going to take me for a checkup on Feb. 7."

"What? Why she want to do that?"

"She said my underwear didn't look the same. She said it looks like I've been having sex."

"Naw, your mother needs to stop her mess."

"I know! It's just going to be more trouble."

"Surely is!"

"I want to go to the doctor when you go."

"Momma probably won't let you."

"Yeah, you're right. Well we will talk later."

"Okay!"

Chapter 9

The Big Day

My mom walked me to the bus for a few more weeks. I had no choice but to get on the bus. After making it to school, James would be out there to pick me up. He would drop me off in time before the bus leaves in the afternoon. I wasn't afraid anymore. I knew this was my only time I could spend with him. I also knew I was hurting myself in school by not coming.

"James, I am sick."

"What's wrong?"

"I keep throwing up."

"What? Are you hungry?"

"I throw up if I don't eat on time."

"Naw! Are you pregnant?"

"Nope, I hope not."

"Well, let's go get something to eat now."

"Okay!"

Before I knew it, I asked James to stop the car. I had to throw up that yellow mess. It always burned as it came in my throat. I hated that taste. We went to get something to eat at Burger King.

"I still felt sick. I probably should have eaten on time."

"Baby, you need to go to the doctor."

"I know. My mom is taking me on February 7."

"What she taking you for?"

"A checkup!"

"Wow!"

"Momma said I probably have a cold coming that's why I'm throwing up."

"Yeah, you probably do." James went and got a room.

"Baby, I really miss you a lot. Did you miss me?"

"Yes, sweetie!"

"How much?"

"More than you will ever know."

"Show me then." I gave him a big hug and a kiss on the cheek. He wanted to go further.

"James, we can't have sex today."

"Why not?"

"I got to go to the doctor, remember?"

"Yeah, you will be done closed up by then."

"Are you sure?"

"Yes, sweetie!"

We had sex for about three hours. James and I took a bath after having sex. We stayed at Knights Inn until school was out. It was time to go and catch the bus. He dropped me off at school. I had to run in order to catch the bus.

My mom wasn't waiting at the bus stop today. That was a miracle. I didn't know what kind of trick my mom was playing. I knew I wasn't going to fall for her trap. I went straight home. I walked in the door.

"Hello, Mom!"

"Hey! Are you just getting off the bus?"

"Yes! Why you didn't come to the bus stop to get me?"

"I'm giving you another chance now."

"What!"

"Okay! You know you'll go to the doctor tomorrow."

"Yes, ma'am."

"You ready?"

"Sure!"

My heart was beating so fast. I was so scared to go to the doctor. I still had confidence that the doctors couldn't find out if I had sex or not. I walked in the room to go do my homework. After I did my homework, I went to sleep.

The next morning, I got up bright and early. I was ready to go to the doctor.

"Mom, I have a doctor's appointment this morning."

"Okay! What time is it?"

"It's 7:00 a.m., Mother!"

"Let me get up now! We have to be there by 9:00 a.m."

"Okay! I'm waiting on you."

"Get your brother and sisters dressed for me. I have to drop them off at school."

"Yes, ma'am."

I got everyone dressed. It only took me thirty minutes to do all this. I felt as if I had to vomit. I ran to the bathroom. I threw up the yellowish stuff again. Maybe I caught the bubble guts. *I am so nervous right now. I'm just ready to get this situation over with.* I ate a bowl of cereal to ease my stomach. By the time I got finished, my mom was ready.

Momma dropped my sisters and brother off to school. We finally made it to the clinic. I used to go in the green door.

"Mother, why are we going in the blue door?"

"Your doctor's appointment is in this door this time."

"Wow!"

We sat there for about forty-five minutes. I began to get more nervous by the minute. The doctor called my name.

"It's your turn, get up."

"Mom, can you walk ahead of me?"

"Okay!"

"You guests may enter room 3. I need you to urinate in this cup all the way up to the third line. Place the cup in the little door."

"Okay!"

"I also need you to undress from your waist down when you come back in the room. Place the sheet across you when your finish."

"Yes, sir!"

I did everything the doctor asked. The doctor took a long time to come back in the room.

The whole while the doctor was gone, my mom tortured me.

"Taquasia, you better pray you are still a virgin."

"I am, Mom!"

"If you're not, I'm going to beat your ass all the way down Sixth Avenue."

"Wow."

"You better tell me now."

"I am a virgin."

When the doctor came back in the room, he had a nurse with him.

"Are you ready, young lady?"

"Yes, sir!"

"Place your legs into the slots. Slide to the bottom of the bed."

I did exactly what he asked me to do. "What are you going to do with that metal piece?"

"We use that to check your cervix." As he inserted the duck head into my vagina, I started screaming. It felt as if he pinched my meat in the inside.

"Girl, that didn't hurt," replied the doctor. "You are fully opened."

"No, I am not, please try it again."

"I'm going to beat your ass, Taquasia."

"On top of that, Carmen, she is pregnant."

"You all are lying on me. Momma, I can't believe they're lying on me."

"You think I'm a fool. Nobody is lying on you. Who broke your virginity? James?"

I didn't say anything. I was busted like a sweet pea. I didn't know what to say at all. We left the clinic. My mom beat me all the way home. She wanted James's phone number. I wouldn't give it to her. She said, "I have sources. I will find out the information I need." We made it to the house. I lay on my bed crying.

This man said I'm pregnant. I'm only in the eighth grade right now. I wondered what she had up her sleeve. "I am very disappointed in you, Taquasia."

"I am sorry."

"That's all you got to say. You're grounded for a whole month. We are not keeping a baby. You are too young."

I called Jaliya. She hadn't gotten home yet. I needed someone to talk to. I called James.

"Baby, I had a bad day."

"What happened, sweetie?"

"I am pregnant."

"What? What your mom said?"

"I can't keep it. I am too young, she said, to have a baby. She tried to get information on you. I wouldn't give it to her."

"Wow, baby! Thanks!"

"You're welcome!"

Chapter 10

The Betrayal

I moved from Florida to Georgia. I visited Florida often. I missed my best friend Jaliya. Most of all, I missed James. We lost contact with each other. I didn't see James until 1997. I had graduated from high school. We were happy to see each other. He was shocked that I had a son. We talked for a long time. He took my son and me to the park. It was so romantic. We were like two peas in a pod. The only thing about it was I wasn't staying that long. We walked to my stepfather's house. I didn't see him anymore after that.

The next time I heard from James, he was locked up in prison. I looked his name up on the Internet to find him. James was facing two life sentences. Throughout the years, we became closer than ever. We fasten and prayed together. We kept in touch through good and bad times. We kept each other motivated. James sent me special cards I could never forget. One was called Prisoner of Love, and the other was Just the Two of Us. One evening James called.

"Baby, I want to ask you a question."

"What is it, James?"

"Will you marry me?"

"Who, me?"

"Yes, you, baby."

"Yes, I will."

"Baby, can you wait on me until I get out?"

"Yes, I will, baby."

"I am moving to Georgia with you. Are you ready for that, sweetheart?"

"Yes, I will wait on you."

"I'll be out soon, baby."

"I love you. James."

"I love you too, Taquasia."

"Sweetheart, get your house in order before I get there."

"I already have my house in order. I know who I want to be with. I have loved you since I was a little girl. Nothing can ever change the way I feel about you."

"All right, baby! I hear you."

James wrote me a letter two months before he was getting out of prison.

Baby, I'm getting ready to get out of prison. I will be moving up there with you. Let me know what you want me to do.

I wrote back to let him know that, I'm still waiting on him. I got no response. James had moved to another prison, and my letter never reached him. After waiting for six months, I finally got a phone call from James. James called me and told me he was out of prison. He wanted to see me bad. We hadn't seen each other in years. I rushed back to Miami only to find disappointment.

James led me on for several months. He kept telling me he wanted me to move back home. He kept asking me to marry him. He also wanted me to have two kids from him. I agreed to marry him since it would have been both of our first weddings. Since I had so much love for James, I would have done just about anything he wanted me to do. I didn't mind having his kids. My cousin called me and asked me, "Was James married?" I told her, "No. He asked me to marry him." I did my own investigation on the computer. It said Mr. James Lyons got married two months after getting out of prison. James betrayed me by getting married to another woman and leading me on. I asked James if he was married, and he replied no. I even had my best friend Jaliya to ask him on the sly. He still replied no with a sneaky smirk on his face.

James hurt me to the point I couldn't eat or sleep for months. The love of my life betrayed me to the point I can't love or trust another man. He acts as if it doesn't bother him. There are many guys wanting to be with me. My heart is scarred. My wounds will never heal. I have never been hurt like this before. After all the hurt and pain James put me through, I have forgiven him. Even though I am finally closing this chapter on Mr. James, we still remain friends.

The end.

AUTOBIOGRAPHY

My name is Tabitha R. Mathis. I was born in Miami, Florida. I was raised in Homestead and Florida City, Florida. I moved to Cairo, Georgia in 1993. I was raised by one parent who is my mother. Her name is Eva Mathis. My father is deceased.

I have four beautiful children Quintavious Mathis, Quaiesha Mathis, JaQwaiveyon Mathis, and LaKwambria Mathis.

I attended Fannie Turner Head Start, A. L. Lewis Elementary School, Homestead Jr. High and Campbell Drive Middle. I also, attended Homestead Senior High until 1993. I graduated from Cairo High School in 1996. I also graduated from Penn Foster College on Jan. 20, 2010.

My mother was a single mother. She inspired me to be the best mother I can be.

I am a single mother and I love it. I have made the best of it.

I was a member of the Zeta Phi Beta Club, Library Club, 4H Club, Safety Patrol Captain, and Sage Club.

I attended Greater William Chapel Freewill Baptist Church in Homestead; Florida1989-1993.Bishop Willie L. Scott was the pastor. I was the captain on the youth usher board. I attended Beulah Missionary Baptist Church from 1993 until 2000. I am now a member of Friendship House of Prayer in Cairo, Georgia. My pastor is Rev. Elder Addison Sr. and Betty Addison (deceased).

My family and I now reside in Albany, Georgia.

www.ingramcontent.com/pod-product-compliance
Lightning Source LLC
Chambersburg PA
CBHW020406290526
45785CB00005B/2450